MW00366284

www.marketingdoctor.tv

People Buy Brands
Not Companies

Published
January 2010
by
Five Titles Press
276 Fifth Avenue
Suite 1001
New York, New York 10001

ISBN: 978-0-9844367-0-5

Printed in the United States of America

10 9 8 7 6 5 4 3 2 1

What They're Saying About John Tantillo,
a/k/a The Marketing Doctor:

"A marketing genius and visionary."
   - Bill O'Reilly, The O'Reilly Factor

"A marketing whiz."
   - Cashman Peters, NPR's Marketplace

"You're the best at this."
   - Neil Cavuto, Fox Business News, to Dr. Tantillo
   on air concerning his Marketing Analysis of Health-
   care Reform (7/22/09)

*"If you want to know how to define and enhance your
brand, you need the marketing doctor, John Tantillo."*
   - Alan Colmes, The Alan Colmes Radio Show

People Buy Brands... *Not Companies*

PEOPLE BUY BRANDS
Not Companies

───────────── Table of Contents ─────────────

A Welcome from the Marketing Doctor

Once I was like a lot of people who think that marketing is just a way of convincing people to buy a whole bunch of things they don't need. Those guys at Procter & Gamble were half magicians/half conmen in my opinion, wrapping whatever it was they wanted to sell us in pretty paper and plastic, putting a jingle on the radio and turning it into pure gold. Yes, I was in the marketing-is-about-creating-need camp.

Then I started studying psychology, and some-where along the way I began to realize that while I wanted to help people, I didn't want to listen to them drone on about their problems all day. Clinical psychology was out. Anyway, I was a data guy, a research psychologist, and I was learning a lot of interesting stuff about how the human animal works. Then, one day, I decided to dip my toe in the "dark side," marketing, and it turned out to be the best thing I have ever done.

When my teacher, Dr. Dorothy Cohen, began to speak I had one of those "aha!" moments that come too infrequently in this life. One of those moments where you say to yourself: "Wow. So that's the way it is." If I can give you a tenth of that feeling in this book I will have succeeded, because what I walked away with changed my life and I've been doing marketing ever since. Dr. Cohen made it simple: You can't create need no matter how hard you try. You can only discover the need and then find a way to meet it. Marketing, she said, was a way of giving people what they needed not what you wanted to con them into buying. In that moment I saw that I could still help people, because I could do it as a marketer.

Now don't get me wrong. I'm not naïve. I'm a New Yorker after all. Do I think some marketing is bogus? Absolutely! But I call that bad marketing (or, even better, promotion posing as marketing). Let's be honest. The fact is that you CAN package absolute crap, promote the hell out of it and make it successful —at least for the short run. Take the Rosenthal Effect (also called "the Pygmalion Effect"), explored in a psychological study done decades ago, that showed that expectations of success in classroom performance on the part of teachers led to higher results in the students for whom those expectations were higher going in. There have even been studies (Jeff Biddle, University of Michigan, and Daniel Hamermesh, University of Texas at Austin most notably) that suggested that the looks of job candidates had a marked effect on employment prospects. Not a surprise. Life isn't fair and humans are biased toward bows and ribbons. Sure we like the nice packaging and can be misled by it!

But, you know what, the buyer can't be misled forever. The marketing I became fascinated by was real marketing, the genuine article, the extraordinary science of meeting human needs. When Fed Ex launched its now legendary "When it absolutely, positively, has to get there overnight!" campaign they weren't creating a need, they were filling one that people had long had —the need for a dependable, overnight carrier of things they needed to send. Fed Ex's slogan was more like an announcement: "hey, that need you have… well, we're here to fill it and fill it better than anybody else can." And, wow, did they ever!

In a perfect world of perfect instantaneous communication where every need was known and immediately met you wouldn't need many elements of marketing like promotion, advertising, publicity —heck you wouldn't need a lot of things! But what we've got instead is marketing and all its parts and it's a pretty amazing way of determining human need and satisfying it time after time, whether it's for the best car, the most reliable phone or a great drink.

One aim of this book is for you to have your own great awakening to the wonders of marketing and branding. To see them through fresh, unjaded eyes and see how the power of the product, service or person can be discovered and marketed to make really amazing things happen.

There's a bit of Carl Sagan in me. I'm a crusader for the big, visionary take of the marketing cosmos.

What I mean by that is that I believe that marketing is involved in just about everything from our personal lives to our political lives to our consumer and professional realities. There simply isn't anything that can't be analyzed more effectively or run more efficiently and profitably when you apply the marketing lens.

Marketing at its best is about making things happen in the world through creativity, intelligence, and adaptability, things that would never have happened had someone not had the vision or the drive to market.

Together let's reclaim the marketing concept from the snake-oil salesman and the high-priced Madison Avenue advertising agencies and their staffs of would-be novelists who in their quest to be oh-so-artistic frequently forget their own brands and the bottom line —they are there to help their clients sell.

Marketing is a science and an art, but it has always been about selling and that, folks, is a very good thing. The bottom line of the marketplace doesn't demand beautiful or witty Superbowl ads that cost some company three million dollars and are over in thirty seconds, the bottom line demands that the customer's needs are understood and served. If this doesn't happen then forget long-term brand success. I'm a former professor so I can say these things, but marketing is really just selling with a college education.

Selling isn't a bad thing and it certainly isn't an easy thing. You need as much help as you can find. Getting people to give you their hard earned cash is part art/part science but its not hocus pocus or trickery. It's the tough work of discovering what consumers might need and determining how best to satisfy this need. Fact is, the best marketing is inventiveness combined with great research skills. Not surprisingly, one of the first things I learned in that marketing class was that Procter & Gamble, one of the best marketers in the world, isn't a marketer first, they're a manufacturer. Research psychologists like myself don't take a step without the data and neither does Procter & Gamble.

I'll talk more about the details of P&G's approach in a little bit, but one thing jumped out for me that day and in the days that followed: a brand is one of the closest things to magic on this earth. Tantillo, what are you talking about? What I'm talking about is that when you've got a success-ful brand things just happen. It's not that you don't have to work hard to make it successful and keep it successful, it's just that in many ways a great brand sells itself. It was the "magic" part that fascinated this research psychologist turned marketer and I've spent three decades puzzling out just how branding works and why it works as well as it does.

So that's the context for this book and our marketing mission, but the essence of this book is clear from the title: people buy brands. Everything in this book is here because it drives home the point that selling is always about customer's needs and that successful brands are, in fact, those needs captured in tangible forms. A company might have a corporate culture, it might have a mission statement, it might even have its own brand (in a looser manner of speaking), but it is the brand they sell (i.e., their product or service) that the buyer is seeking and that's what we're going to focus on here.

This book is designed so that you can drop in, drop out or stay a while by reading it straight through (I've even done something a little different

—and user-friendly— by including a short glossary of terms up front so that you know they're there and can either read them now or go back to them whenever you want). Most of all, the book is designed so you learn something explosive, hopefully mind-altering, likely business-changing on every visit to these pages.

The Marketing Doctor's Glossary

Adpublitizing

The creation of an advertisement that is sure to generate controversial coverage, thus ensuring that the advertisement and the related brand get many more impressions than a typical media buy.

Celebrity Brand

A sub-class of the personal brand (see "personal brand"). The celebrity brand has some interesting elements such as the effect of faddishness on its development.

Core Product Features

The immediately identifiable characteristics or functions of a product or service that distinguish it from other products or services.

Narrowcasting

The opposite of broadcasting. Narrowcast is essentially the way web-based advertising and interaction works: you tailor and target your message for a specific audience. It can also be thought of as a kind of niche marketing.

N.A.V.

A three-letter term intended to capture the fundamental characteristic of a brand as a function of marketing. The name of the brand is the noun. The adjective is the best description of the brand. The verb is the active promotion of the brand. N.A.V. is the Marketing Doctor's acronym to help people understand that a brand is a dynamic thing that must have all three components in place to be successful.

Personal Brand

A person seen through the marketing lens and understood as a brand with core and related features.

Poli-marketing

The process through which a politician identifies the real needs of the voters and then sets about to address them whatever it takes. This process is inherently different from merely "stumping" in that it requires a conscious marketing approach (i.e., development of brand consistency) and especially requires a balance between flexibility (i.e., reading the polls) and stability (i.e., staying true to one's core features).

Pull Strategy

A promotion/sales tactic that harnesses a brand's direct appeal to the consumer in which the consumer takes the initiative to seek out the brand. The opposite of push strategy (see below) since the marketer appeals directly to the consumer. This strategy works especially well in the Internet context, where buyers, voters or other members of a Target Market seek out and buy or support the brand that meets their needs.

Push Strategy

A promotional/sales tactic that aims to push the consumer, the voter or other member of a Target Market to buy your product, candidate et cetera by having a third party literally push your product on the Target Market by incentivizing more sales (i.e., third party receives a dollar amount for each push product sold, typically in the form of a commission).

Related Product Features

The packaging, the colors on the box, the typeface and other external elements. Related features can be dismissed as the "superficials" but Tantillo emphasizes the word "related" and shows how for successful personal brands, like successful commercial brands, related features are the bridge to the Target Market. The packaging tells us what the core features are all about.

Target Market

The group of people who most need or want your product or service. These are the people you must never forget, ignore, or think that you can live without. These people are the lifeblood of your business.

The Marketing Concept

The essential role of marketing as a vehicle to identifying and satisfying consumer needs.

Why Superbowl Advertising
Is a Waste of Money

I've talked and written about Superbowl advertising being a waste of money for a long time because, frankly, Superbowl advertising is the poster child for the concept that people buy brands, not companies.

Well, economic realities (and maybe a little bit of my counsel) have finally begun to shake conventional wisdom up and we're seeing some long time Superbowl advertisers like Fed Ex and GM take a pass in recent years.

In a fractured media market and a troubled retail environment taking a pass on the Superbowl makes more sense than ever because single, one-trick-pony advertisements simply don't do marketing well.

That said, there's still more hype than there should be and advertisers are still lining up to pay big bucks for a very questionable return.

One Superbowl advertiser that recently did it right in 2009, though, is Jeffrey Katzenberg and Dreamworks. In fact, this cutting edge guy and his cutting edge company suggested one way that Superbowl advertising can work for an advertiser.

To compete with falling DVD sales and ever more sophisticated in home viewing options, Katzenberg and others (i.e. Cameron and Avatar) are pioneering the next generation 3-D theater

How did the Superbowl fit? Katzenberg identified the event as the perfect marketing platform for the launch of this new 3-D experience and brought people a taste of the new 3-D directly to their living rooms.

Dreamworks did Superbowl advertisement with a difference. They weren't really doing an ad as much as offering an event (their 3-D launch) within an event (the Superbowl).

This is real marketing. It's not an advertisement,

it's a sales promotion. This is not the "watch it and hope that they buy product" model; this is give them the experience (i.e., sampling, the most effective way to sell product) and then let them know that there are future events (movies) that they can participate in.

This is marketing as the new advertising and advertising as part of a strategic web of message delivery and experience that re-enforces brand and generates sales by meeting the needs of a Target Market. I didn't think I would ever say this, but sometimes a Superbowl spot might just pay.

But here are the fast facts for why Superbowl ads are usually a terrible way to spend money:

1) The most famous ad in Superbowl history — Apple's "1984" ad directed by Ridley Scott of Gladiator fame— became an icon and introduced so-called "event marketing"... But for Apple it spelled the beginning of the end in its personal computer war with IBM and Windows. In fact, in the year following the big Superbowl ad, Apple sold fewer computers than ever.

2) Not everybody watches the Superbowl. The same Superbowl money spent on ads to reach those watching the other television programs on at the same time could land almost double the viewers in the 18-49 demographic.

3) Why does the hype continue? Because Superbowl advertising is great publicity for advertising agencies (unfortunately, it's a poor business decision for their clients).

4) A direct marketing campaign for a website or product that spent $3 million in advertising and production costs combined would generate a much higher multiple of sales.

5) The cost for one Superbowl ad in 2008 (somewhere between 2.4 and 2.7 million for a 30-second spot) could buy up to 600 30-second TV ads in the NY market or 800 30-second TV ads in LA.

One company that has decided to take a miss on Superbowl advertising after years of participation is General Motors, the lucky recipient of the latest government lottery drawing (i.e. corporate life support). GM has begun putting their brands first and now seems to be using good marketing sense when it comes to this question. GM is bypassing the Super Bowl and other big-ticket ad buys in favor of a sponsorship maneuver with a much smaller audience (narrowcasting again). Last year, they sponsored the Glenn Close vehicle Damages (it was tagged, "Commercial-free, courtesy of Cadillac.")

There are so many ways to slice a marketing budget, why do it with an expensive exercise that puts company ahead of brand?

P&G — A Company Is Never Greater Than Its Brands

If there is one company that has defined the nature of brands and shows us how true marketing works, it must be Procter & Gamble.

P&G was started in 1837 and made a lot of its money in the 19th century from its candle business. Needless to say that had that been their only business, then P&G would not exist today.

But ultimately P&G is a company that knows that people buy brands. It has survived and prospered because it knows that companies must never be in love with themselves, they must be in love with their brands. Don't get me wrong, P&G is a great company as far as companies go (they introduced a profit-sharing plan to all employees in the 1800s), but what sets them apart is their slavish devotion to their brands. They're a company that owns, develops and innovates many brands and it was this company that responded to a profound shift —the death of their first core business (i.e., candles)— by mastering new markets as they emerged. By 1920 they were out of the candle business and inventing the "soap" opera for radio —an incredibly inventive and effective way of promoting P&G products to mass audiences the world had never been able to reach before. Today, the company has revenues of almost has revenues of almost 75 billion dollars annually and spends 2.5 billion advertising in the United States.

P&G invented the soap opera as a way to reach its Target Market by capitalizing on the emerging radio and television industries.

One of the reasons I respect P&G so much is that they are the masters of creating and controlling their brands. Soap operas made sense because they were essentially a creative platform that could highlight their packaged goods and build brand loyalty. Soap operas were and are controllable since P&G was literally writing the scripts and micro-managing the talent.

There are a few soap opera standout performers, but for the most part the stable of actors and actresses do not become brands in themselves. This is the result of smart management. Sure there was Luke and Laura's wedding on General Hospital, but the horse pulling the soap opera cart is not a personal brand, it's P&G, the reason for the entertainment's existence and the soap opera stars' paychecks. It's ironic that the emotional rollercoaster of soap operas was one of the most dependable platforms for brand development and promotion.

The great thing about products is that they don't have personalities —at least, not personalities that can go off script and do stupid things on their own. You can add personality and energy to the packaged good by creative association and present it in the best possible light (i.e., the soap opera) and that's what P&G has been doing for years. The soap opera model might be faltering now because of changing tastes and viewing habits, but P&G is already moving into new ways of reaching their

Target Markets through music ventures and direct Internet marketing. They will ultimately succeed even if soap operas die, because they will remain flexible and responsive to the times.

P&G does brand management better than anyone —after all they wrote the book and have survived and thrived era after changing era. They are terrific proof that marketing —far from being superficial and after-the-fact— can be at the center of a successful business model. That's right... Marketing is a foundation to build a business on. P&G knows that the current market will be tough for some time, but their products span the gamut from high- to low-price (P&G has its own discount brands for those consumers who are going to belt-tighten down from more expensive items). P&G's products are always built with marketing in mind... A creative idea is always market-tested, and if it fails that test then it doesn't become a product. End of story.

Which brings me to Pringles...

Everything You Ever Wanted To Know About Pringles (But Were Afraid To Ask)

When Procter & Gamble wanted to get some market share in the crowded potato chip market they set to work the way they always do.

P&G knows that you can't create demand. You can only discover a need in your Target Market and then discover the best way to satisfy it.

You see marketing, and by extension branding, is about being aware of reality. Whether it is the reality in your workplace, your marketplace, yes, even your friendships or marriage. Marketing is real and the best marketing is an active engagement with reality.

Back to Pringles. Why those cans? To protect the "chip." I put chip in quotation marks because a Pringle —as some of you may know— isn't technically a chip at all. It isn't completely made of potatoes. It is a crisp. A snack designed to meet a distinct consumer need that P&G discovered through exhaustive research.

So what did P&G discover?

They discovered that a significant number of people complained that when they bought their potato chips, opened those fresh bags, more often than not, half of their chips were broken. P&G saw their way into the market. The Pringle was born. Everything else followed from this.

Enter Frederic J. Bauer — Fred was a pretty anonymous guy.

Bauer was an organic chemist and a food storage expert. He designed the Pringles can. The crisp delivery device. He was very proud of it. Some of Bauer's ashes were even buried in one.

I want to underscore three things here:

One, the cans were only one portion of the exhaustive work that went into developing Pringles.

Two, committed people like Bauer were involved

in the product creation from beginning to end.

And three —and most important—marketing drove the creation of this product and marketing was based on the consumer needs and desires that P&G discovered.

P&G is, first and foremost, a marketing company that understands that marketing encompasses manufacturing —marketing is that foundational. They invent what people need or want. They don't find ways to create needs or wants, because this company —that has been in business for over 150 years —as I said earlier, they used to make most of their money from candles—knows that you can't create needs and wants —and, because this is crucial, I want to repeat myself— you can only discover needs and wants.

That said, I hate Pringles. But P&G —nothing personal— doesn't care what I hate. Why? Because Tantillo is not the Target Market, people who care about broken chips more than eating 100% potato chips —they're the Target Market and that's who P&G cares about. The kind of Target Market that would appreciate that P&G used a super computer to help design the chip shape so it would not fly off the assembly line and break.

There's something else to learn from P&G and Pringles. Initially, though, they hit a lot of resistance from their biggest competitor, Frito-Lay. The good folks at Frito-Lay went after Pringles for its ingredients and its taste. To be honest to this day I can't eat a Pringle because I'd much rather have a potato chip, broken or not, than an unbroken Pringle.

P&G never did knock Frito-Lay out of the Number one chip-making spot with Pringles, but they did establish a one-billion dollar in revenue a year global brand and they did it by listening to the needs of a particular group of customers.

Newspapers and Television Must Rediscover Their Brands

Newspapers and television. Like the supposed fate of arctic glaciers, this media bunch is collapsing faster than anyone predicted and a focus on companies to the expense of brands is at the center of the problem.

Newspapers first. The Christian Science Monitor ended its existence as a printed newspaper and went exclusively online last year. The New Jersey Star-Ledger cut 40 percent of its staff. The New York Times keeps making newsroom cuts. The Rocky Mountain News was shuttered after 150 years.

What in the name of William Randolph Hearst is going on here?

Basically, ad revenues are falling for newspapers on the print side, and growth in online ads isn't making up for it because no one can seem to sell online ads for the same amount of money that they could sell print ads.

As a result, many of these newspapers find themselves in the strange spot of having more readers than ever (online), but making less money.

Television's in terrible shape too as the recent flap over Conan O'Brien and The Tonight Show underscore. No one knows how to battle the effect of DVRs, hand-held on-demand viewing, and YouTube.

From a marketing point of view, I think we're seeing a once-in-a-generation re-alignment in advertising models that might very well make two media (television and print publications) unprofitable businesses (or much less profitable businesses).

In other words, every so often something changes in the marketplace that translates to a radical shift in what a business considers valuable as far as advertising is concerned and what a business will pay for it. I'm a longtime proponent of the value-for-my-money advertiser crowd. Advertising should generate sales. Period.

Television and newspapers are both suffering from the same thing: too much choice, ease of access and questions about the value of the kind of advertising they do (thanks in part to the more targeted advertising models introduced by the Internet).

Fact is, you can have a top quality product, even a hugely valuable cultural product like great journalism or great entertainment and it can be a poor driver of sales —such a poor driver that it is no longer economically viable to produce.

Let's continue to take a closer look at newspapers. Newspapers were able to get away with ignoring their Target Markets for years. In the beginning (i.e., the 19th century), the most successful newspapers were called "penny dreadfuls" and they knew what their Target Market craved (lurid news stories) and delivered it at a cheap price.

Over time, newspapers evolved into what we have today (pretty large and all over the place in terms of content and approach); and to a certain extent many readers bought them not to read but out of a kind of obligation, a sense that somehow they ought to have a newspaper around.

It's not just about declining readership or increasing newsroom costs or even being innocently caught unaware of the change to their industry... Newspapers never got real marketing —the real marketer can be hurt by big marketplace upheavals, by the way, but they won't ever be completely surprised— or, rather, they got real marketing at the beginning (think Hearst and his nineteenth century penny papers), but then lost it once they became "institutions."

Newspapers simply assumed for far too long that the worst case scenario could not happen to them since —like The Rocky Mountain News— they had a long history, a profession that heaped awards on its practitioners and a false belief that the daily newspaper was an inevitable feature of big city life.

Any one of us who aspire to real marketing can learn from this. One of the biggest dangers for any brand is a sense that it is inevitable and the neglect of your customer's needs that comes from this sense of inevitability. A real marketer must always assume that a better job of serving his/her customers' needs can be done —and be actively figuring out how to do that better job.

This dynamic is changing fast, and as a result circulation is dropping. Add to that that online advertising can't generate the same kind of money that print advertisements did and you've got trouble.

I don't really see what newspapers can do to become marketing winners other than to focus increasingly on their Target Markets' needs. I think you're seeing this online in the way that newspapers are bringing their readers into commenting on pieces and doing social networking via the site.

But will this save the big, traditional newspaper (whether national or regional)? I don't think so.

What we'll probably end up with is fewer newspapers both online and in print, smaller newspapers (in length and number of staff) and a greater emphasis on content that is highly targeted to readers' tastes and when/where these readers read.

If there is a newspaper future, it will be one driven by smart marketers such as urban newspapers Metro and AM, which can be read in less than thirty minutes (the average subway commute), are highly targeted to the city dweller, are given away for free and can still charge good rates for their advertisements.

This is where people buying brands not companies come in. Any newspaper that remembers that its brand comes first (not the inevitability of its company) will seek ways to maintain its brand (e.g., a reputation for quality) while discovering new ways to reach its Target Market.

Kindle might very well be a life-line for newspapers, but only newspapers that learn what their brand is and how best to deliver what their Target Market wants will be able to exploit the technology of the new platform.

It's also possible that for some newspapers, online is not the answer. One community newspaper in New Jersey made a decision several years ago to stick to print. It was the TriCityNews of Monmouth County, New Jersey.

At the core of their decision was —you guessed it— how to best serve the needs of their Target Market and still turn a profit. Their decision was to offer competitive advertising rates and then do everything in print and not give any content away for free online. The result has been profitable. Advertisers like it because the model works for them and the paper can remain a going concern.

But there's more to learn from this operation. Let's remember the buggy cab manufacturers. When the car market began to develop, there was still a need for buggy cabs, but not enough for Fisher Body, a leading manufacturer, to continue to grow in the same way. What did Fisher do? It joined forces with General Motors and started to make cabs for cars. Fisher realized that the fundamental feature of their brand was not horses, but cabs. It didn't matter if the compartments were being propelled by horse or engine.

What's the connection between Fisher Body and a small newspaper in New Jersey? It's this: always remember the brand you are selling. This newspaper is selling local news and information, and that is what creates a valuable platform for its advertisers. It needs to stay local and stay small to stay strong as a brand because its roots are in the community it serves, and that community is what makes it relevant and profitable.

Bottom line: the Internet wouldn't add value to their product — at least not yet. Just because you can put all your content on the Internet doesn't mean you should if that's not how you're going to reach your Target Market. By the way, you can argue that this is where Gannett has made a big mistake with its model. In the quest to find big balance sheet "efficiencies," they've forgotten the value of being micro-local, even though that's the kind of product their regional newspapers ought to be providing (and the product the newspapers they took over traditionally offered).

Interestingly, when you use the brand not company model as a guide what seemed to be a very different business from newspapers, I'm talking about television, suddenly isn't so different.

So let's talk about Hulu.

Hulu. The video website that lets users watch TV shows and movies with 42 million visitors a month recently inked a deal with ABC/Disney to host its shows. ABC is now the fourth of the big broadcast networks to have taken an ownership stake in Hulu.

According to The New York Times, it has only taken Hulu 18 months to become the third most popular video site on the web.

I've said it before, but it bears repeating: the new marketing is going to have to happen on many levels and in many places all at once in the ever more challenging pursuit of a fragmented Target Market. We've seen that with the Superbowl question and it's true of television in general.

That said, I think Hulu's success is more than just an interim step in trying to make money from a television-viewing audience as it transitions to the web. In other words, I think Hulu's success is showing us something about one aspect of future marketing on the web: the importance of the surrounding environment (read, content) for advertisers who are concerned about their brands.

Jeff Zucker, president of NBC Universal an investor in Hulu, said something very interesting in that Times article. Here it is: "Advertisers have made it clear that they want a safe environment unpolluted by videos of cats on skateboards."

This might just be whistling in the dark —after all, any network guy would love to be assured that the viewing environment created by a tried and true network brand has a place in our wild new web world— but I think there's some truth here.

Namely, advertisers who care about their brands really do care about where and how those brands meet the Target Market and Hulu is offering a polished, network-style showcase that will allow television content to make money from advertisers and advertisers to have their products and brands promoted in strategic and controlled ways.

Hulu looks like it might be an answer. But let me stress this: unlike the past, there isn't going to be just one answer. The issue may be that intrusive advertising is finished and we are witnessing the rise of the social-networking model in which we choose the advertising we want rather than be "forced" to encounter the advertising we would not choose.

The Times hints at this by stating that CBS, which has not joined the Hulu wagon, distributes its shows on three hundred video sites. Three hundred —that's a lot of sites. And even though ABC is joining Hulu, it's not going exclusive —they will still be airing shows on their own website.

Bottom line: we are probably witnessing the emergence of one of the platforms that marketers will use to reach their Target Markets, but there is still a lot of "old media" thinking that has to be gotten past.

In fact, even the NBC debacle over The Tonight

Show is more about the death throes of old media than it is about a genuine mistake. If anything, Jeff Zucker was probably ahead of his time when he shook up the prime time line up by getting rid of very expensive entertainment programming and replacing it with Leno and his talk show. At the time of the shift, this was my marketing assessment:

Moving the current Tonight Show host —still at the top of his game in the later time slot and format— to prime time represents nothing less than the kind of programming anarchy that you had back in the infancy of television... only back then, TV executives were discovering how to harness the incredible commercial power of a new medium. Now, as television fades, they're trying to figure out how to squeeze out the last bit of juice. It's called narrowcasting.

Basically, narrowcast is the opposite of broadcast. Narrowcast is essentially the way web-based advertising and interaction works: you tailor and target your message for a specific audience. It's also called niche marketing.

Obviously, broadcasting is preferable because it

has the best shot at reaching the largest number of people in one fell swoop. The only problem is that as technology has changed (cable television, TIVO, the Internet, et cetera), the idea of a captive audience is basically gone, as are huge audiences all watching the same thing.

My guess is when the business history of the last twenty years is written, people looking back will be amazed at how long it took for advertising prices to go down on television (both broadcast and cable). Wasn't it obvious, I can imagine a future historian asking, that more outlets competing for an ever smaller and less captive audience should have meant that rates should have been pushed down quickly in response?

Basically, I think it boils down to this: Television was so powerful for so long that even bottom-line thinkers didn't recognize that its best days were behind it as a marketing tool. It's also possible that the bottom-line reality that demands showing a return on investment might have been clouded by the same era of easy money that colored many bad business decisions over the last 15 years.

In other words, just like big advertisers traditionally

didn't question the value of Super Bowl advertising, they didn't question the value of a big ad buy on television.

So, again, what does all of this mean for the marketer and advertiser? It means that prime time is soon going to be a shadow of its former self and that narrowcasting, or niche marketing, will become the standard.

Whatever happens with NBC and the other networks, what we'll probably see happening relatively soon is less new prime-time-style entertainment content (because the money just won't be there for production costs) and also more of the old-fashioned kind of corporate sponsorships we used to see as well as narrowcasted work (sponsorship is terrific because it allows a brand to dominate the viewer's attention without competition). But that's what real marketing is all about... figuring out who your customers are and then letting them know how you are going to meet their needs. It's about a living brand and not some blind allegiance to an unchanging and arrogant company.

Gourmet!
How You Spoil
a Great Recipe

Not too long ago, Conde Nast announced that it would stop publishing Gourmet Magazine after seven decades. At the time of the announcement, the magazine had over one million subscribers.

The outside consultants who prompted this decision argued that Gourmet would still maintain its brand equity despite shuttering the magazine. After all, they could use the brand name all over the place: on a website, on branded merchandise, on co-branded television programs. You can almost hear them saying, "Talk about win-win!"

Save us from this kind of "win-win" because it's

just the old cost-saving, bean-counting lose-lose using branding as lip service.

Here's why.

The formal definition of a brand is a "name, term, symbol, or special design that is intended to identify a product."

This is fine as a starting point, but I want to introduce you to a better way of understanding a brand.

I call it the N.A.V. concept. It stands for noun, adjective and verb. This is how N.A.V. works: the name of the brand is the noun. The adjective is the best description of the brand. The verb is the active promotion of the brand.

Basically, the consultants are making the mistake of thinking that a brand is only the name. This is a huge (but common) mistake. The problem? By confusing the Noun or name Gourmet with the whole brand, they're focusing on only one-third of what makes the brand great.

The other two-thirds —and this is the lesson for anyone concerned with their own brands— are being ignored.

What's the adjective in Gourmet? It's the core

features that readers came to depend on and highly value.

By core features we're talking about the magazine's reputation for testing and re-testing recipes, the superb quality of their editorial board and staff, the cumulative knowledge and know-how that comes from running a top magazine for seven decades. And, by the way, don't forget their subscription base of over one million. With respect to the Gourmet brand, these people are part of this brand's great features. Just the same way that everyone is talking about the equity in social-networking, your long-time, loyalist clients/subscribers become part of your brand.

When Conde Nast shutters Gourmet, all this gets lost.

Finally, the verb part of the brand.

Without the high quality content and know-how, what do you have to promote? Nothing. They can push the name Gourmet until the cows come home, but they've kicked the legs out from under the brand and in time the name won't mean all that much.

This is a classic example of people forgetting the brand (i.e., the magazine) and promoting the company (Conde Nast).

When was the last time you hit a newstand ready to buy any magazine as long as it was Conde Nast? I think I just heard you say "never." People buy the brand, not the company.

Apple and Microsoft —
A Tale of the Brand-Loving
Company And the
Company-Loving Brand

Over the years I have written extensively about two tech companies that I think almost perfectly sum up the difference between a company that markets brands and a company that markets itself. I'm speaking about Apple and Microsoft.

Sure the fact that a product is made by Apple gives the consumer confidence, but since consumer's buy brands, not companies, this aspect is not the deciding factor. The product is the deciding factor. Some evidence of this with Apple is, of course, the products that they have produced that have flopped (e.g., Newton). But Apple has never dwelt on its failures and because of this and the fact that the company always picks itself up and gets back to the drawing board, we remember it for its successes.

Not so with Microsoft which had enjoyed such marketplace dominance that its real marketing, people buy brands, approach atrophied long ago (if it ever existed at all).

In analyzing these companies, I've made a few observations that shed light on just how a company can either profit from or ultimately suffer from putting its products and Target Market first or not.

Let's look at Microsoft first.

Microsoft's brand image has been damaged by years of a you-must-like-our-products-or-else approach. Customers accepted this because they had little choice. Now that this reality has changed, we have seen the gradual slipping of their bottom line since profits are no longer assured by their market dominance.

How toxic is Microsoft's brand image? Here's a good example. Microsoft's Vista struggled to gain market share not because of the weakness of Vista itself. In fact, Vista seems like pretty good software. Apparently, one focus group overwhelmingly liked it when they were told that it wasn't Microsoft's Vista —and they were shocked when they learned the truth.

This is an example of how years of disregarding the product brand can virtually guarantee the defeat of subsequent products, regardless of their quality. Even though people buy brands first, the company's brand matters since in the ideal situation, it is the company's reputation that supports the consumer's confidence in purchasing the product (of course that reputation must be based on a track record of great products, products that the Target Market loved).

The good news is that Microsoft might be beginning to show signs that it understands that the consumer comes first and you simply cannot follow a "build-it-and-they-will-come" approach. They have announced a plan to open Microsoft retail stores to enable them to interact directly with the consumer (and have already begun opening them). They have even hired David Porter, formerly an executive at Wal-Mart (they know marketing), to oversee the effort.

This is hopeful news and might just suggest that my old poor marketing exemplar is finally realizing that real marketing is about understanding your Target Market and satisfying needs —not just delivering the "brilliant" product vision with the message to the consumer: take it or leave it (but you'd better take it).

The former Wal-Mart executive will probably push real marketing, but we'll have to wait and see if this transforms the company —after all, Gateway computers tried the retail store approach, and that failed. Still, it seems promising since they are taking a page out of Apple's book on successful stores and seem intent, based on their public statements, to cultivate relationships with customers that will lead to better and better products.

If this initiative leads to real marketing juices flowing through the corporate veins, then we might just see a rebirth as a company that has learned to put its brands and Target Market first.

So if Microsoft has faltered, how has Apple managed to do the opposite (especially over the last decade)?

Well, besides a dedication to developing products that people want, another part of putting the brands first as a company is being very adaptable to the environment and keeping the company arrogance temperature very low. If your corporate culture is about the flow from the Target Market back to the company and not the other way around this will inevitably translate into great product development and great company development.

Last year, Apple gave us an excellent example of this when Cartier sued them over two applications for Apple devices that it said violated Cartier copyright. Apple immediately withdrew the applications from its stores. Cartier promptly withdrew its lawsuit.

This didn't become a business-hurting situation, because Apple didn't let it. The company responded immediately. Part of being a company that is able to put brands first is the ability to readily make course corrections. When an airplane pilot flies from New York to London, he or she has to make many course corrections simply to stay on course. Winds, the curvature of the earth and dozens of other variables mean he or she must remain responsive to change. Between Point A and Point B, the only straight lines in this life are the ones we make by our vigilance and adaptability.

A healthy company is constantly making these

course corrections, and the key is responding promptly and correctly to evolving realities. This same corporate approach is evident in Apple's brand creation. Like P&G, Apple puts its consumer's experience first and consistently builds products based around what people want, like and need.

This approach is supported by another Apple characteristic: openness to having its products improved by its users. Apple has built devices that other people —i.e., programmers and users— have added even more value to by creating applications. Apple doesn't want to micro-manage this independent creation because it will douse the creative spirit and the accessibility of its product. The risk is that copyright infringement happens— but it's a risk that Apple can counter by being responsive when problems arise.

An arrogant company could have become embroiled in a legal morass with Cartier; Apple is too smart for that. Real marketing is built around a sophisticated and "living" dyad —a two-directional relationship between seller and buyer that is predicated on satisfying needs on both sides. The dyad is alive, adapting and moving at all times.

Let me leave you with a story about Microsoft — a story that I can't imagine ever being told about Apple. A woman is suing Microsoft for being charged nearly $60 to downgrade —that's right downgrade— from Vista to an older version of Windows because Vista had so many problems. Put the brand first and this kind of thing would simply never happen. Oy vey!

How To Brand
[FILL IN THE BLANK]
In Thirty Seconds

Now for something completely different, an extra, if you will, some practical and specific takeaways you or people you know might be able to use right away. The list of "brandable" things and activities is almost endless, but the principles are consistent and applicable across a wide-range. To prove my point and give you a few usable examples, here are four:

How To Go Brand Your Job Interview!

So you've landed the big job interview. Congratulations. You know the job interview how-to basics. You've got the right clothes, you're ready to offer the firm handshake (but not too firm); look the interviewer in the eye; send a thank-you note afterwards; your resume's crisp and letter perfect ... but before any of this you've got to go brand yourself! Why? Because the competition's going to be using the "how to" interview basics, so you need the branding edge to ace that interview.

Branding isn't just about setting yourself apart from the competition ... it's also about figuring out what sets you apart from the competition. It's about figuring out who you are (and who you're not) —this is your brand, after all!— and how to best express your brand.

Most important, you need to figure this out before you walk through that interview door. A great outfit and a decent joke are good to have in your interview "toolkit" but if you don't know your brand —well, it's over before it even started.

Getting to know your brand takes a little market research. To do this, here's the Marketing Doctor's Four-Point Inventory:

1. What one word do you think best describes your brand? Are you "creative," "detail-ori-

ented," "on-time," "friendly," "reliable?" Give this some serious thought and try to come up with that one word that really captures your brand —trust me, you're gonna get a lot of mileage out of this one! One guideline: go for the "bigger" word. Example: Are you just "punctual" or are you "punctual" because you're "detail-oriented" — given a choice I'd pick "detail-oriented" because it applies to more things and says a lot more about your solid work ethic.

2. How do people close to you describe your brand (family, friends, colleagues)? (Hint, ask them!) Here, don't restrict them to one or two words. Let them loose on your brand and be prepared to listen. It might not be easy for you or them, but there's real treasure to be found here. This is what I like to call a real-life focus group!

3. What one thing do you like about your brand? Dislike? Again, like #1, target exactly the right like and dislike. Do you like that

your "detail oriented?" Why? Is it because you put a lot of value in getting things exactly right and doing a good job? Similarly, what do you dislike about your brand? You run late? Well, maybe this is something you want to change, but this also might be seen as a strength. You run late because you're always giving full attention to whatever it is you're doing at a given time and forget about the clock. In other words, you don't cut people or jobs short because you have somewhere else to go.

4. What one thing do people close to you like about your brand? Dislike? Same as #3, except here you're more likely to get some real surprises (you'll be doing this at the same time as #2 by the way). People will say things you would never have expected both good and bad. Take a lot of notes!

Now that you've got a picture of your brand in your head use it! Here's how:

1. Put that one word that describes your brand into a sentence in a way that applies to the job you're interviewing for. Example: Your word is "goal-oriented" and the job is sales. Here's a sentence: I'm a goal-oriented person and I won't be satisfied until we've beaten our numbers.

2. Get used to referring to what people close to you have said that they like about your brand. Let it guide you on how to present yourself. You might even weave some of their observations directly into your interview. Expressing others' viewpoints and perspectives on your brand shows your interviewer that you're sociable and open to collaboration and other people's input. A plus for any potential employee.

3. Use what you like and dislike about your brand to your advantage. Emphasize the positives, but be prepared to acknowledge some negatives about yourself to the interviewer. Doing this will show that you're not

someone who thinks they walk on water. Many employers are looking for people they can groom and grow in the position and the company. They don't want perfect. They want real!

4. Like #3, use what others like/dislike about your brand to your advantage. Suppose someone surprised you by saying you were "relaxed in a good way" even under pressure. That's a positive that you might not have recognized on your own. Similarly, for the negative. What if someone said that they thought you had bad table manners. Wow! That's actionable, especially if your job interview's happening at lunch. You might be surprised what you find out —both good and bad. Whatever it is, use everything to strengthen your brand.

The bottom line is that like it or not, you've already got a brand. Learning more about that brand and harnessing its power will give you a real edge over people who don't know anything about theirs!

How To Go Brand Your Wedding!

Folks, weddings can be branded and it's time for the Marketing Doctor to tackle the how tos of Wedding Branding.

Fact is, preparing for a wedding is a great time to think branding! Afterall, a wedding is literally going to create the marriage of two great brands. You and him/her!!! And like everything about your personal brand(s), a wedding has got to start with you.

In so many ways a wedding has always been about branding whether people have thought about it this way or not! The couple chooses colors, fabrics, locations, designs... I mean, they might as well be hammering out a logo —and, of course, they basically do this in the invitations (Wow, talk about a direct-mail campaign!).

There's been a lot of talk about how expensive wedding's are getting. According to an article in *Money*, the average wedding is costing upwards of 30 grand these days and www.costofwedding.com lets you calculate let's you calculate wedding costs and even gives you averages for your neck of the woods.

But the Marketing Doctor is here to give you some branding basics that will go a long way to making your wedding: 1) even better with branding and 2) probably end up costing you a lot less. Here goes.

As with personal branding, you and your soon-to-be spouse need to sit down and do an inventory. Who are you exactly? Be honest and thorough! Do this individually first —remember this is a coming together of two brands so you better get an idea of these individual brands first!

What do you individually really like (list it even if it sounds crazy!)?

Who do you individually really like (this is your day! Why ruin it with people you don't like?)?

What do you want this day to individually express?

You're going to be surprised by what you discover about each other and this is great (at least I hope so)! Next, do these questions for you as a couple. More than likely you're going to find out that both of you are going to have to compromise a little —and the Marketing Doctor knows better than to get involved in that one (good luck!)!

At this point, you should really have a pretty good sense of what your combined brand is and this knowledge should guide you through the obstacle course of wedding planning (e.g., location, photographers, flowers, food, dress, etcetera etcetera). Basically, rather than do a one-size fits all approach, your branding knowledge will allow you to take control of the process and even make it fun! Not everyone needs flowers! Not everyone needs a spring wedding (especially if you met in the fall or winter)! Not everyone wants formal! Not everyone needs a twenty-course meal fit for a Maharajah! Maybe you want to dress up like characters from Star Trek or say your vows as you and your betrothed parachute to earth! You get the picture! Knowing your branding essentials will allow you to say "Yes" and "No" with more confidence and might even lead you to have one of those weddings that everybody talks about —in a good way! And if you're true to your brands, I'm confident that you're going to be better hosts to your guests!

Some relevant family Tantillo wedding history. I can remember the battle my sister had with my mother on who to invite to hers! My sister wanted something small. My mother wanted a Godfather-sized wedding with all the cousins and every generation! Many things may have changed in wedding planning in 30 years, but these kinds of tussles have stayed the same! Also, more on the one-size-doesn't-fit-all point. My sister was very practical. Her wedding gown was bought on sale, because the retail store was closing their bridal department —a four-figure dress for three-figures! Boy, she was one happy bride, and my brother-in-law one happy groom!

And let me leave you with this bit of trivia. Did you know that the most expensive wedding ever was thrown by Lakshmi Mittal on June 22, 2004? The six-day celebration of his daughter's nuptials came in at a mere 60 million dollars!

How To Learn Marketing From The Shopping Cart

I've been feeling a little confrontational lately picking at some of the branding missteps of some big brands, so I want to step back to "how to" marketing basics with —of all things— the shopping cart.

All of us take the shopping cart for granted, but before 1937 it didn't even exist! If you wanted to carry things around a store you lugged them around in a basket. Then Sylvan Goldman, a successful self-service retailer, realized that people would have a better experience in his stores and buy more things if they had a cart. He made the first one out of a folding chair.

Recently I've been thinking a lot about how to market products that fulfill needs that your Target Market doesn't even know they have. These days we call it guerilla marketing —outside the box thinking about getting your Target Market to embrace your products. Fact is, smart business people have been doing guerilla marketing all along!

Goldman did it with the shopping cart. He saw a need and sought to satisfy it but at first there was a hiccup. No one used the carts! His guerilla marketing answer: hire models to use them in the stores. It worked. His customers saw how the carts worked and copied. The clinical psychologist in me stands up and applauds Goldman's insight into social pressure and the marketer applauds the idea of rolling up your sleeves and actually teaching your Target Market how (and why) to use your product! Shopping carts caught on fast after that! But that isn't the end of the story. The next two decades saw the evolution of the shopping cart into the current version that could carry a child and for the singles without child could use that space for extra merchandise carrying. Other refinements were the extra space underneath for more stuff and that they stacked into each other to save floor space. Talk about doing research — this is marketing at its best!

Yes, research! People sometimes say to me: it seems that all you're saying is do research. And, fact is, they're absolutely right! But there's a twist. Research isn't just some throw-away concept that means I can't bother to give you a specific answer! Research is about being engaged with your customer and going to bring you the facts that will give you the answer.

There is never a one-size-fits-all answer to a marketing question —anyone who tells you that doesn't know what they're talking about. Research is an art and a science (boy, did I say that?)! And, usually, the answer that research gives you is simple rather than complex (marketing types like to call it the parsimonious explanation)! Like the shopping cart you start with the observation that there is a need that you can probably satisfy. Then you figure out how to satisfy that need. But, really, that's just the start for any brand. A successful brand is always reaching out to its Target Market, observing and listening to what it wants and needs and then making brand "course corrections" both large and small in response. Research is what gives you reality. Good marketing isn't smoke and mirrors —it's the exact opposite. Cutting through the smoke and mirrors so that you can profit from the reality.

Like Goldman and the shopping cart, research is about observation and acting on your observations again, again and again!

How To Brand The New Grad

The difference with new grads and branding is that in a way you are making decisions now that will arguably position and define your brand for the rest of your life. This is a tall order and not one size fits all —it never does when we speak brands!

And like any fundamental how to, the best bet is for me to supply some rules of thumb and let you run with them:

1. You're a brand whether you want to be or not. This means that you have certain core characteristics that are on display as I write this and which those people you encounter —friends, family and potential employers— recognize as being a distinct brand. The catch is that your real brand might not be being expressed as well as it could be. The good news is that you can do something about it and you will have the rest of your life to perfect it!;

2. If you are not in control of your brand then you will not be in control of your life. Hopefully you will learn this early: that if you don't care about your brand no one else will. This may be a sad fact but it is true. And this also pretty much goes without

saying but I'll say it anyway: if you are not projecting your true brand then people will be responding to something that you aren't.

Say you are a hard worker but don't reflect this in your clothing or manner so it remains unknown. Chances are that the opportunities that would tap your hard working nature just won't materialize because hardworking is not something people think of when they think of your brand. I can't tell you the number of times people have told me they pay close attention to details and yet they looked like they just got out of bed or they say they are good with project deadlines but are always running late to meetings — hint, they might really be good with project deadlines but their chronic lateness at meetings raises doubts in a potential client's mind and that client may never give them that chance to prove how good they are at hitting the deadline (in this case, stopping the lateness is the best way to show the brand's time-oriented strength) ;

3. Marketing is not evil and it is not superficial. Marketing and branding is about figuring out the core features of a product or service and then using the best way possible to let other people —specifically your Target Market— learn about and come to depend on these features. Your life can become a learning experience in marketing;

4. The first step in taking control of your brand is to learn about your core features. Your core features are those features that make you who you really are;

5. Learning about your brand's "core features" takes research and what I call a "brand review" (those of you who have read the job interview how to can skim what comes next or, if you want a refresher, go through it a second time);

6. The brand review I use with my clients is very involved and customized but here's an example of one basic brand question (and

potential answers) that can help anyone kick off a Brandover: What one word do I think best describes my brand? Are you "creative," "detail-oriented," "on-time," "friendly," "reliable?" Give this some serious thought and try to come up with that one word that really captures your brand —trust me, you're gonna get a lot of mileage out of this one! One guideline: go for the "bigger" word. Example: Are you just "punctual" or are you "punctual" because you're "detail-oriented" — given a choice I'd pick "detail-oriented" because it applies to more things and says a lot more about your solid work ethic.

7. The most important thing you can do as you set out to learn about and build your brand is to get "fearless." By this I don't mean reckless... I mean courageous in a smart way: don't be afraid to ask people what they think your brand is; take the answers constructively not destructively; be prepared for your brand to fail and be prepared to figure out why it failed. And if you fall, pick

yourself up, brush yourself off and keep going;

8. Be prepared to wait —patience is a virtue, especially when you know that you have a solid brand. This is counter-intuitive from a young perspective, but believe me be patient! Brands build slowly and just because everything doesn't happen at once doesn't mean its not going to happen. Once your brand plan is in place give it time to work;

9. That said, don't give it too much time. Time waits for no man or woman. If you're not getting the kind of response you'd expect from your brand then take a step back and consider what might be wrong. Remember, people will rarely tell you what they don't like about your brand —i.e., why they're not buying it!— so you've got to listen carefully to what they are and are not saying. And you've got to ask questions along the way and be prepared to change course if you need to; and

10. Finally, as you set out to determine and then build your brand remember that a "just the facts" approach is critical. In this case, less is definitely more! A short list of features will help keep your focus better than a long and uncertain one.

When you head out the gates of whatever fine institution has seen fit to let you loose onto the world, remember that those basic core features of your brand (who you really are) deserve to find a place where they will be most at home, best used and, lest we forget, happy! So, part of the process might include trying on a few different hats before you find the one that fits your brand. This is called brand research —specifically finding the best Target Market and positioning for your brand— and the most important thing is to be aware that the career you were sure wasn't for you might, in fact, be exactly what your brand needs! And from there always stay open to the changes in the marketplace and be ready to reposition!

Learning the Science of Brands through the Lens of Politics

My mother told me to never talk about politics (or religion) in polite company. But I will do anything in the service of spreading the word about marketing —the marketing that I know and love. I've had the opportunity to train the marketing lens on politics for my work over at Fox Forum, so here are a few posts that should amply illustrate how marketing works in the political context. In these pieces, I used the science of marketing to show how to show how in politics as with everywhere else, following the laws of brands is critical for clarifying what will work and what won't in the political arena.

So if you can please put your own personal politics aside —I know it's a big ask— and prepare to see politics in a completely different way (if you can't, I won't be offended if you decide to skip this part altogether).

I'd like to start with one post that I'm pretty proud of —it seems eerily predictive (but it's not hocus pocus or psychic powers, it's marketing):

The Democratic Brand Is In Trouble
And It Doesn't Even Know It Yet
February 18, 2009

With pride there is a fall and there's an even bigger fall if you are proud for all the wrong reasons, especially when those reasons include mistakenly thinking someone else's accomplishments are your own.

This is the biggest problem facing the Democratic brand today: taking credit for President Obama's success.

Brand Obama's accomplishments are Brand

Obama's. They are not the Democratic party's. If anything, for Candidate Obama to become President Obama, the Democratic party was as much or more of a stumbling block than John McCain. Fact is, when Obama was railing again Washington on the campaign trail, the Democrats were in charge on Capitol Hill and part of that railing was directed at them (and the people loved it).

Brand Obama knows the difference between his brand and the Democratic party. As a consummate brand manager you can bet that he's going to take every opportunity to underscore that difference.

In fact, he did exactly that this week.

When President Obama signed the massive new stimulus package into law this week, he held the signing in Colorado not Washington. Now that's a message that the Democrats had better not ignore — the stage wasn't cluttered with politicians.

Brand Obama is proclaiming (just like Brand Reagan did) that he is not of Washington and that he is taking action with the people and for the people. He's saying "It's not about you politicians in Washington; it's about us folks in the heartland and what we need."

(That said, he's got something else big in his favor. If this stimulus fails, he can throw Congress under the bus by blaming them for originating it ("I had to sign it because we had to do something!"), but if it succeeds, he'll get the credit.)

That street runs only one way. The Democrats are not Teflon, Obama is and Obama is a poli-marketer not a politician.

I've been talking about poli-marketing for the last few weeks and I want to take a moment to clarify what I mean by this term.

Poli-marketing is not just a slick way of saying politicking; it is a complete departure from politicking.

Old-style politicking just won't work anymore, because people aren't going to put up with it. After decades of marketplace choice and with the rise of an ever increasingly interactive Internet, they want and expect results from their government.

Here's what I mean:

Politicking equals meeting voters' perceptions in order to stay in power. This has nothing to do with satisfying real needs and everything to do with controlling the way things are perceived by the voter.

It is also issue and ideology-based meaning that the politician says what people think he or she wants to say. This is like putting a product on the market before test marketing it and shaping it to genuine needs —a bad idea.

But Real Marketing —which is the foundation for poli-marketing— equals discovering real needs and then satisfying them. In poli-marketing this translates to a politician identifying the real needs of the voters and then setting about to address them whatever it takes. It's simple —move from the issues-based politics of the past to needs-oriented politics.

Success in politics is performance-based like never before because President Obama's victory gave the electorate a renewed sense that they had power to change their government. I'm not saying all the old political realities are gone, but the ratio of poli-marketing to politicking has shifted distinctly in the former's favor.

New York's Michael Bloomberg was one of the first poli-marketers. It doesn't matter if he's a Democrat or a Republican, he made it known from the beginning that he was there to serve the real needs of real New Yorkers whatever ideological or issue-related toes he has to step on or borders he needs to cross.

Mayor Bloomberg has the luxury of seeming to stand apart from politics (heck, he can always leave and return to his billion dollar lifestyle) and so does President Obama (whose political career — mythically or not— seems to have begun almost reluctantly).

Not so the Democrats who are seen as professional politicians who live or die on what comes out of their mouths and what direction the wind is blowing. These old-style politicos are going to get a drubbing in the weeks and months to come.

Look at Roland Burris raising the specter of corrupt Democratic politics and the whole raft of ethical problems that confronted cabinet selections. Or the entire State of California sinking under debt and an obstinate Democratic political machine.

Now you have the possibility that the Democrats are going to run some kind of "Truth Commission" to scrutinize the Bush years.

Wow. What a terrible idea.

Who exactly is calling for this move? The

American people? Hardly. This is old school: when you've got the upper-hand you stick it to the other guy and bet on the voter not caring or noticing. This is not needs-oriented and so the Democrats must drop this because it is a risk a political party cannot afford to take today.

My guess is that President Obama is going to reject this idea outright and decisively. He's got to, because even the most solid brands have limits and an investigation of a prior president by a sitting president could badly wound his brand since it could not help but be seen as a partisan act.

The Democrats would do better with the following basic approach:

1) drop all thoughts of re-visiting the past (accept President Obama's advice and look to the future and solving the problems of the American people);

2) generously give President Obama the victory in the stimulus and get behind him across the board (don't jostle for the spotlight);

3) give him support in his mortgage plan and go a step further by insuring that Republicans can get firmly on board this one;

4) hit the road, get out of Washington and show that Brand Obama has opened their eyes to poli-marketing and that their concern is the American people and not inside-the-beltway squabbles.

This will neutralize Brand Republican by taking away Brand Republican's greatest strength: its role as a check on big, left-leaning, one-party government.

The Democrats need to do this now, because the American people are going to choose harshly if the country is mired in partisanship two years from now. We'll see the tables turn faster than anyone can believe right now. Democrats must come to the realization that the American people did not vote for them, but against the Republicans (because the Republicans did politics the old-fashioned way, they ignored real needs).

A year later and that last post seems to be coming true. The morale: ignore your Target Market, think company (in this case, party) and not brand (i.e., a party elected to serve the stated needs of the electorate, your Target Market) and you'll be sorry. Now for the Republicans (I'm an equal-opportunity analyzer). I still stand by the basic conclusions of the next piece, but admit it seems that they are having a bit more success at the polls than I would have expected (but, again, I'd lay that at the feet of the monumentally bad choices made by the Democrats). So without further ado:

Don't Hold Your Breath, The Republican Brand Isn't Going To Get Its Act Together Anytime Soon.
February 26, 2009

Folks, I've been talking about the Democrats so much lately that I'm guilty of neglecting Brand Republican...

Unfortunately, Brand Republican is guilty of the same thing.

Bobby Jindal's shaky response to President Obama's Tuesday night speech is just the tip of the branding iceberg. Apparently Republicans were some of the harshest critics of his speech...

What in the name of Ronald Reagan is going on here to this venerable brand?

Essentially it's this: the Republican Brand is in a deep brand crisis. This is not the kind of brand crisis that comes from losing a few elections, making a few tactical mistakes, falling asleep at the political switch.

Nope. This is the kind of brand crisis that comes from a cumulative loss of brand identity, strategy and implementation. Make no mistake: This is the kind of crisis that can sink a brand.

Here are some of the reasons why I am convinced that the Republicans aren't going to get their act together anytime soon no matter how badly they want to:

There are no standout figures in the Republican Party who are unifiers (Note: as of this book's printing, Scott Brown looks like he might be emerging as one). While there are several prominent "brand" representatives, none of them are comprehensive enough to unify the whole brand in a Reagan-like fashion. Jindal's problematic performance drives this point home and also drives home the related point that Republican's are almost too desperate for a standout unifying figure and this desperation is leading to the too early anointing of leaders.

The next Republican brand leader has to be unifying and even more important develop organically out of great personal/political strengths of an individual who meets the needs of the party and people;

In fact, many prominent Republicans are actually rejecting the party openly while remaining in it like Schwarzenegger this week on ABC who relished the fact that the Republican Party was against some of his initiatives. This falls under the category of "A brand divided against itself cannot stand.";

The Republicans are being reactive not proactive. The appointment of Michael Steele to lead the party while perhaps a good choice as far as Steele's qualifications and character are concerned appears to be a reactive choice since it seems a superficial response to another African-American's (Obama's) electoral success. Also, Republicans have appeared to have been reacting to Democrat initiatives in the legislative process. Bottom line: a growing brand is proactive not reactive;

Republicans are in disarray in their beliefs and principles. Lindsey Graham seems about to argue for bank nationalization —something which even some Democrats think is too much government. Also, Jindal said he wanted to reject Fed stimulus while Schwarzenegger and others want to accept it;

Recent history in Britain gives us a sense where this will go. Blair took the steam out of the Conservatives there by agreeing with many things they advocated. They became reactive, had no standout figures and have been languishing in disarray for almost a decade and are only now beginning to regroup their brand. (By the way, Tory leader David Cameron is beginning to become that universal political figure conservatives have long sought in Britain —again, a fairly organic brand development (meaning: it takes time and you can't push it);

Republicans lack a clear cut vision of the future. Being the party of NO is not enough. This is like marketing a product because of what it is not instead of what it is. This strategy has been tried before. How about 7-Up... the "un-cola"? 7-Up might have gained some market share at first, but it never managed to gain too much momentum against Coke and Pepsi. Successful brands have clear cut visions of the future that are positive not negative. End of story. Reagan was not so much against big government as for small government and the wherewithal of the American people to make good choices if they were just left alone to do it. With a positive brand vision, consumers/voters know where the brand plans to go and grow and because they know this they become a part of the brand's growth through their support; and, finally...

As a result, we might also be witnessing the end of the Brand Republican and possibly one of those rare moments in American history when a third party emerges. It's not impossible folks. Sometimes a brand simply can't be saved. Have you used Oxydol lately? Probably not. But Oxydol was once one of the most popular detergents of the 1930s —one of those "inevitable" brands that dominated the market-place. No brand is inevitable or unsinkable in either the supermarket or at the polls —think about the

Whigs. When Abraham Lincoln saw the writing on the wall about this increasingly "oppositional" party that was simply unable to build consensus, he left to join the newly formed Republican Party. Then a few years later Lincoln left the Republicans to run as a member of the National Union party in his second term.

That last point aside, not all the branding omens bode ill for Brand Republican.

That was true, not all the omens were bad. I still believe that the Republicans must replace the negative rejectionist instinct with a positive platform, but the energy for this kind of change is there and they are thinking about the brand and their Target Market more than the Democrats at this point.

Is President Obama The New Coke?
March 12, 2009

Folks, first some history. In the early eighties, one of Jimmy Carter's bright young political advisors, Pat Caddell, landed the plum marketing gig of guiding Coca Cola into the future —he almost ran that venerable brand aground.

I'm talking about the New Coke debacle. Threatened by Pepsi's increasing market share and driven by marketing data that said that the consumer wanted sweeter drinks, Coca Cola scrapped its time-honored soda and introduced New Coke.

The outrage was deafening. People couldn't believe that their soda was being taken away from them. Coca Cola listened and New Coke is now just a distant memory.

How could all of the polls, surveys and consumer data have been wrong?

Well, they didn't take into account what really mattered to the consumer: choice and continuity. One more thing —and it's a biggie— Coke was thinking about cola drinkers not Coke drinkers. It forgot its Target Market.

So I ask: is President Obama the New Coke?

The electorate seemed to want change in 2008. President Obama seemed to represent the change they wanted. This change was about politicians moving beyond partisanship to get things moving in Washington —it was not about big government solving everyone's problems. It wasn't a Democrat or a Republican that the electorate wanted. No, it was a person of change who would not put the same old practices into political play.

In the early eighties, the cola consumer seemed to want change too, but when they got change, they didn't like what they got. The people drinking Pepsi didn't start drinking New Coke and Coke drinkers stopped drinking the New Coke. This is the worst possible marketing outcome for any product or political brand — you end up pleasing none of the people all of the time.

There are two basic scenarios for Brand Obama at this point.

One, the electorate thought they were getting one thing in President Obama and instead got something very different. In other words, they wanted the change he said he would bring, but dislike the change he is actually bringing and actually believes in. In this scenario, President Obama is what he is and simply won't be able to adapt to what the Target Market demands —this spells one-term president.

Two, President Obama is the change the electorate wants and is capable of embodying this change, but he has lost sight of his Target Market's needs and is becoming a victim of inside-the-beltway realities and left-leaning pieties and interest groups.

This is the New Coke scenario. Instead of subtly altering the ingredients of the product to adapt to changing tastes, you make a big product change, bring people's attention to that change and alienate your Target Market. Go ahead and do that Mr. President —but only if you want to squander the marketing success that brought you to the show and got you elected POTUS!

The problem for Brand Obama is that once you become the New Coke, it's very hard to become Classic Coke again. Every compromise, every pork-filled, partisan program, every pro-big government, anti-free market message drives his brand farther and farther from the Target Market that elected him.

Presidents Reagan and Clinton both knew this about their Target Markets: the American people could be stretched, but in the end poli-marketing was the order of the day: Americans' fundamental needs and beliefs could not be forgotten.

Even though these men came from opposite ends of the ideological spectrum, as a poli-marketer each president remained true to the fundamentals of the American electorate that has always believed in basic fair play, the power of individual freedom and the limited uses of government.

These first 100 days are tricky for all presidents. In this short testing period, Kennedy went a long way to losing the south to the Republicans for a quarter century.

But if Brand Obama doesn't want to stay the New Coke, he must make some strong statements that drive home that he is not merely more of the same liberal Democratic brand.

There are some signs of hope for his brand. This week even as he signed the stimulus package, he criticized its earmarks and said that going forward this pork would not stand. Better still, he should have vetoed that bill and re-enforced his change brand with his Target Market the electorate.

A few days before that, he even implied that he's going to take on the powerful teacher's union to deliver on his promise of improving our education system. That's big and if he actually does it we might just be spared another New Coke.

Stay tuned.

Well we've been staying tuned, but it's hard at this point to see that the New Coke mistake has been corrected. If anything, they're pushing the product even harder.

Tantillo's Four-Point Brand Take Away

Because people buy brands, not companies, brand integrity must be a foremost concern. Obviously bad things can happen to brands despite your best intentions and good contingency planning (although most of the time, the twenty-twenty of hindsight will show those places where a brand foundation had some cracks). So here's a quick four-point take on what happens and should happen when your brand runs into trouble.

1. The worst way to make a major brand decision is out of desperation. If you don't absolutely

have to take action then don't. Sit on your hands. Avoid the temptation to panic. Instead, take a breath and proceed to step #2.

2. Remember the Tylenol crisis. Perhaps no other event in the history of marketing is as meaningful for the "marketing in desperate times" category. The Tylenol poisoning could have easily destroyed that brand, but instead of letting this happen, the marketers took a step back and considered the core values of their product. They recognized that the poisoning could have happened to any over-the-counter medicine and that nothing fundamentally was wrong with their brand. This was not a time to rebrand and lose existing marketing share, but a time to make a brand adjustment —take the lead in consumer safe packaging— and then promote the hell out of the brand. The strategy proved hugely successful and Tylenol expanded market share beyond pre-poisoning levels.

3. If your brand is facing a crisis, either large or small, the first step before changing the name or other important elements is to assess what hasn't changed. A brand is not built up over night and successful marketing is never an instantaneous event. Neither is the destruction of brand value instantaneous. If you have gotten far enough along in your business, most of the time the crisis is external. Perhaps the market is changing or your message is missing the target audience. If the crisis is external, a temporary drop in customers because a new dry cleaner has opened shop and is giving away free service, and you overcorrect then your long-term success may be hurt.

4. Most crises are a long time in building and the best way to insure against them is to have a regular Target Market reach out. Even small businesses can design a seemingly informal way of learning exactly what their customers like and don't like about a product or service and then making small brand adjustments in

response. Marketing and branding at best is fact finding and then taking action based on the fact finding. You can't do good marketing unless you know the facts.

What Makes A Great Personal Brand?

In much the same way that people buy brands (not companies), people buy a celebrity brand. And when I say much the same way, I really mean it. I want us to stop using the word brand loosely and instead draw the correlations that count. In other words, if a product is designed to serve certain needs, so must a celebrity brand. This is critical. All too often, people —especially celebrities (and I'm talking about virtually anyone, even those only recently flush with their fifteen minutes of fame)— mistake the goodwill of their audience with a license to do and be whatever they want to be.

Wrong.

Just like in product land, parameters exist that dictate just what a celebrity can and can't do if they want to maintain their Target Market and hopefully grow that Target Market. How many times have we seen a teenage performer (e.g., Miley Cyrus) wrongly think that the seeming universal adulation means they can "branch out" (e.g., in Cyrus' case, have provocative photos taken for a magazine)? The same thing happens to entertainers (e.g. Bono) who think that their success on stage means that they will be welcome on the world stage.

Bottom line, personal brands that fail have forgotten that the brand must come first. They've forgotten what their core business is, who their Target Market is and how to remain true to these two things. What better way to understand this dynamic than to take a look at how the best celebrity brands have achieved what they have achieved?

I've selected eight prominent personal, brands to analyze. Each of these brands is unique. Each is wildly successful. Each has withstood the test of time (except Rachel Ray, but my guess is that she will and besides she's a great example of the chops your brand needs at the start of that long career).

You might not like every single one of these brands, but I guarantee that you can learn a lesson from each one. Most important: There is one common thread that no one should overlook. Not one of the eight was "destined" to accomplish what they did. In other words, what plucked Warren Buffet or Madonna out of obscurity was smart, consistent brand work.

In short, they took their brands seriously and this has made all the difference. That means that whoever you are and whatever you do, you've got a brand that can grow if you're willing to take your brand seriously too.

So without further ado, the top eight:

Warren Buffet

The Oracle of Omaha is considered one of the greatest stock pickers of all time. He is the quintessential value investor and everything about his personal brand says this. His net wealth valued at some 62 billion dollars is the direct consequence of his brand which is all about investing in value rather than hype. He still lives in the same house he bought in 1958 for $31,500 and his word is his bond —a rarity in legalistic America. I came across this quote of Buffet's from earlier this year and, frankly, I think it says it all:

"You can sell it to Berkshire, and we'll put it in the Metropolitan Museum; it'll have a wing all by itself; it'll be there forever," he says at the February meeting. "Or you can sell it to some porn shop operator, and he'll take the painting and he'll make the boobs a little bigger and he'll stick it up in the window, and some other guy will come along in a raincoat, and he'll buy it."

Bottom line: hundreds of thousands of guys started before, with and after Warren Buffet, but there's only one Buffet. Why? Because here's one personality brand that has been consistent and growing since Buffet filed his first income tax return at 13 and deducted his bicycle as a business expense.

You simply have to admire a person who so perfectly embodies his brand and makes you think too. Truly an original.

Martha Stewart

How many high-powered career women have a passion for cooking, catering and gardening? Too many to count. So how did Martha Stewart go from being a stock broker to the expert on all things lifestyle? She knew what her Target Market needed and her brand delivered.

Even when she had her legal troubles she decided "to focus on my salad" as she famously did on the CBS News Early Show in 2002. She was concerned about her Target Market and not external elements that had nothing to do with her brand.

If you remember that interview, the host had asked about the charges against her, but Martha had a salad to make so too bad. Being focused on her salad seemed funny at the time, but being focused on who she is and what she does —her brand— enabled Martha Stewart to stage a comeback that few could have predicted. And it's also the reason that this master of the culinary, home and garden arts has long been considered one of the most powerful women in America. Whatta Brand!

In short, Martha Stewart knew that focusing on charges of stock fraud was not her brand —it was a distraction. She is a grand marketer, not a shrewd financial professional who knew how to play the system —if she was the latter there would never have been any charges of stock fraud.

Her brand like any successful brand is an expression of her — her energy, her attention to detail, and her knowledge about the home arts and a genuine interest in the things that her readers, television audience and consumers care about.

Her recipes work because she is the kind of woman who tests recipes to make sure they work. Take a look at her blog, The Martha Blog at www.marthastewart.com, and you get a sense of just how her brand and her business go hand-in-hand. Even the photo captions have niggling little details (i.e., "Ile flottant or, more correctly, oeufs a la neige with spun sugar.") that tell you that Martha really is focusing on her salad and helping you make yours. I love the Martha Stewart brand.

Oprah Winfrey

Oprah Winfrey is a personal brand and a media empire in one. Does she know what she is doing or what?

Known for her inspirational influence on millions, her own story is inspirational. Born and raised in trying circumstances, Oprah quickly rose to the top of broadcasting by breathing life into a Chicago talk show and basically revolutionizing the confessional type of media approach that we know today.

But she didn't stop there. Oprah is an Academy-Award nominated actress and a magazine publisher. She is ranked as the richest African American of the twentieth century. And she's still going strong as she branches out onto the web (her site oprah.com receives 70 million page views a month). There are only a few personal brands who I hope to meet someday, and Oprah is one of them.

Ultimately, though, her consistent commitment to her personal brand has been what has made all of this possible. Almost everything she has done, whether it was starting and funding a school for girls in South Africa or starting her famous book club is built on things that are close to her heart and resonate with anyone who knows her brand. If her work doesn't make you a little more hopeful, then you'd better call a psychologist for an optimism bypass.

You won't see Oprah leaving her brand behind to

jump into something lucrative that isn't consistent with who she is. The closest she came to this is the Big Give, but even this show was related to her basic Oprah values.

As long as Oprah continues to be Oprah, this brand will grow. I tip my Borsalino to this great brand!

Tom Cruise

The crazy couch incident aside, Tom Cruise is a brand to be reckoned with. Sustaining a top box office career as Cruise has done for almost three decades defies the odds. Add to this his ability to achieve both big commercial success along with critical success and you've got a brand phenomenon on your hands. Now the Cruise brand has moved into serious movie production at United Artists and Edward Jay Epstein, the economist, has argued that Cruise is among a handful of producers who can guarantee billion-dollar movie franchises.

The one take away from the Cruise brand is the importance of smart choices and then total brand commitment to those choices. When Cruise has experienced the occasional flop, he moves on quickly and soon redeems himself and his brand. I say this all the time, but it's easy when you keep marketing in mind and Tom Cruise definitely does. Good work, TC.

Madonna

Madonna is a good artist, but she is a superior marketer —really, a marketing genius. She has an uncanny ability to know what her Target Market likes and she consistently delivers it. This is her "brandmark" if you will.

Another stand out characteristic of Madonna's brand is drive and change. She landed in New York as a teenager with dreams to be a dancer and lived in squalor until she began to realize those dreams.

Her brand is about talent, ambition and re-invention. I'm not sure I can even count how many brandovers, Madonna's had: material girl, the Sean Penn marriage, the movie roles, Like a Prayer, the Truth or Dare documentary, then motherhood, children book writing and wife of Guy Ritchie in the English countryside. And now she's back again with a new brand look that we're only now just getting a sense of.

Whether this time change involves divorce or not, the fact is Madonna has broken back out onto the scene as the masterful marketer she has always been. Her Vodafone concert a few months back in New York and signing with tour company Live Nation instead of her traditional record company showed that Madonna really gets it when it comes to marketing her brand. I've got to say it again, successful brands think Target Market!

Barbara Walters

Barbara Walters makes the list because she wasn't a natural for the medium —television journalism— as it existed at the time and that she ended up conquering. First, she wasn't as glamorous as other female anchor contenders. Second, she had a funny way of speaking. Boy, can I relate!

So what made her brand succeed? She understood her brand's greatest strength: she could identify with people. She was raised in a theatrical environment and from a young age met many celebrities. As a result, she says that her sense of awe of celebrity was diminished. She could approach the rich and famous as people while understanding why other people — read her Target Market— thought they were special.

Walters has made a career and built a powerful brand out of empathizing. She has frequently been criticized for her so-called "soft ball" questions, but it is exactly those kinds of questions that can result in the most surprising answers and have led her prime time celebrity interviews to be consistently among the highest-rated.

She built on her brand by branching out into her own show, The View, which continues to grab viewers and generate controversy and headlines. Through the years she's been lampooned and disrespected by colleagues but Walters has always stuck to her brand by doing work that played to her empathetic strengths and ignoring those who thought she should move her brand into mainstream journalism. Instead, she's experienced almost five decades of success and mainstream journalism has moved closer and closer to her brand.

Steve Jobs

I really appreciate this brand! This dynamic founder of Apple whose brand was eclipsed in a corporate shakeout and has now re-emerged stronger than ever on the strength of his visionary products is one of my favorites.

His brand is about innovation and nothing speaks to the value of learning and taking time to figure out your brand than the commencement he delivered a few years ago. Here's an excerpt:

Reed College at that time offered perhaps the best calligraphy instruction in the country. Throughout the campus every poster, every label on every drawer, was beautifully hand calligraphed. Because I had dropped out and didn't have to take the normal classes, I decided to take a calligraphy class to learn how to do this. I learned about serif and san serif typefaces, about varying the amount of space between different letter combinations, about what makes great typography great. It was beautiful, historical, artistically subtle in a way that science can't capture, and I found it fascinating.

None of this had even a hope of any practical application in my life. But ten years later, when we were designing the first Macintosh computer, it all came back to me. And we designed it all into the Mac. It was the first computer with beautiful typography. If I had never dropped in on that single course in college, the Mac would have never had multiple typefaces or proportionally spaced fonts. And since Windows just copied the Mac, it's likely that no personal computer would have them. If I had never dropped out, I would have never dropped in on this calligraphy class, and personal computers might not have the wonderful typography that they do. Of course it was impossible to connect the dots looking forward when I was in college. But it was very, very clear looking backwards ten years later.

I'll paraphrase the speech as best I can. Basically, Jobs reminisced about his college experience at Reed, particularly that experience that occurred after he had dropped out and was simply taking classes for his own edification. One of these classes introduced him to calligraphy. As a result, he became fascinated by the history of typography. Now, his point was that at the time this fascination didn't seem practical at all. What could he do with this knowledge? Well, ten years later when they were designing the Macintosh computers, all of this learning came back to him and multiple typefaces were integrated into the Mac and as a result of the Mac this became a universal standard for computers.

Jobs' point is a quintessential branding point: everything you do and everything you are can have a powerful benefit for your brand.

Jobs' brand is about loving what you do and this carries over into the dynamic products that are loved by millions. We can all learn a lot both personally and professionally from this brand.

Rachel Ray

Rachel Ray is a brand newcomer and the jury is still out on her brand's longevity. But from the looks of it I think she will be sticking around.

So far she has a similar brand arc to Martha Stewart —but by no means as diverse as Stewart. She's brought her brand focus on delivering simple and effective solutions to cooking to a huge audience and she seems to understand what her Target Market wants. Ray is a kind of blue collar Martha Stewart. She appeals to her Target Market where they are.

Martha appeals to the way they aspire to be.

Her personality brand —down-to-earth and lively— works well with her chosen formats — cooking and talk shows— and should continue to work. With Rachel Ray you want to relax. With Martha Stewart you want to impress. There is room for both.

My only concern is that unlike Stewart who took years to build a brand base and then branched out into multimedia, Ray is doing all of this very fast. That's not always good for safeguarding the integrity of a personal brand (since the temptation with an immature brand is to go for high visibility and big money). Still, this brand is strong and set to grow.

Epilogue

First and foremost, I see myself as a teacher. I prize those moments when I have seemed to reach another human being with my passion for marketing. I hope that this book has served in this cause and that your perception and approach to marketing has been sparked and broadened.

When you see yourself as a teacher, there is also no greater reward than those moments when you can see what progress your students have made and think —hopefully with some justification— that you played some part in their success.

James C. Metzger is one of those people. Jimmy was a student of mine back in the days when I was banging the lectern as a business professor at Hofstra.

I like to think that in addition to Jimmy's natural talents (i.e., a great athlete, a gifted speaker and critically, in my book at least, a singularly good listener), Jimmy walked away from my instruction with a lifelong appreciation for caring deeply about your Target Market, so deeply that you never tire of reaching out to them. Well, however great or small my role in his development, today Jimmy is James C. Metzger, CEO of The Whitmore Group. He is a strong and distinctive brand who is a first-rate marketer in the finest sense of the word, and this translates into one fine human being.

For me, James is an example of the good things that happen when you remain tireless and true to your brand. Hats off to you James and for everyone

who reads this book and applies these principles to their businesses, lives and encounters with the world may the wind be at your back and marketing in your mind.

James C. Metzger with The Marketing Doctor
at a Hofstra University Fundraising Event

Made in the USA
Lexington, KY
22 December 2010